Teen Guide to BUDGETING, SAVING, AND INVESTING

Sara Rowe Mount

ReferencePoint Press

San Diego, CA

Printed in the United States

For more information, contact:
ReferencePoint Press, Inc.
PO Box 27779
San Diego, CA 92198
www.ReferencePointPress.com

LIBRARY OF CONGRESS CATALOGING-IN-PUBLICATION DATA

Names: Mount, Sara Rowe author
Title: Teen guide to budgeting, saving, and investing / by Sara Rowe Mount.
Description: San Diego, CA : ReferencePoint Press, Inc., 2026. | Includes bibliographical references and index.
Identifiers: LCCN 2025032473 (print) | LCCN 2025032474 (ebook) | ISBN 9781678212506 library binding | ISBN 9781678212513 ebook
Subjects: LCSH: Teenagers--Finance, Personal--Juvenile literature | Budgets, Personal--Juvenile literature | Investments--Juvenile literature
Classification: LCC HG179 .M688 2026 (print) | LCC HG179 (ebook) | DDC 332.024--dc23/eng/20250919
LC record available at https://lccn.loc.gov/2025032473
LC ebook record available at https://lccn.loc.gov/2025032474

CONTENTS

Why Learn About Personal Finance?

For Hannah, a college freshman, it feels like money or rather, the lack of it, has been a key part of her life since childhood. "I grew up with a scarcity mentality," Hannah reflects. "I can't remember a time in my life when the world felt stable, or like my future isn't in jeopardy because of some world tragedy." The financial instability of her growing-up years has followed her into adulthood. She worries about how her current choices and fluctuations in the US economy could impact her financial future. "Even deciding what school to go to, it's like, okay, can I afford to pay tuition or take out a loan?" But then, she continues, "you risk losing job opportunities if you don't have a degree."[1]

Financial Stress and Struggle

Hannah's experience is unfortunately similar to that of many teens growing up in the United States. Studies show that the typical American family is struggling financially. A 2023 survey by LendingClub Corporation found that 62 percent of those surveyed were living paycheck to paycheck. This means that if a job loss occurs, these families will likely only be able to pay their bills for a month or less. Many families also have had to resort to using credit cards to pay for needed items or emergencies. A 2024 NerdWallet survey found that 48 percent of respondents were using credit cards to purchase necessities, and a 2024 MoneyWise survey found that 41 percent of those surveyed had credit card debt.

Teens are aware of the stress and worry that finances can cause for their caregivers, and they feel it as well. After all, many families are in situations far more dire than having to cut back on eating out or not buying name brand clothing. Job losses, stagnant wages, and rampant inflation are all having very real impacts on families across the country. Financial struggle may look like facing eviction, having utilities like heating or electricity turned off due to nonpayment, or visiting food banks to be able to eat.

> "Many teens said that they couldn't afford school supplies or that their caregivers worried because they lacked money for necessities. In the months when teens reported experiencing these hardships, they were more likely to feel depressed and get in trouble at school."[2]
>
> —Jamie Hanson, assistant professor of psychology at the University of Pittsburgh

Jamie Hanson, assistant professor of psychology at the University of Pittsburgh, was interested to find out the impact that a family's financial situation can have on teens, so he studied one hundred teenagers in the Pittsburgh area over nine months. "Many teens said that they couldn't afford school supplies or that their caregivers worried because they lacked money for necessities," says Hanson. "In the months when teens reported experiencing these hardships, they were more likely to feel depressed and get in trouble at school."[2]

Financial Future

While teens worry about their families' financial struggles, these struggles also inform how they feel about their own financial futures. Unemployment, shortages, inflation, tariffs, and recessions are all part of the world teens are inheriting. They question how they will pay for college and whether they should take out student loans if they might spend the rest of their life paying them off. They also wonder whether they will be able to find jobs once they graduate from high school or college and whether they will be able to earn enough to pay for their bills and the life they want to live. Licensed clinical social worker Timmesha Butler-Davis has found that stress over money is a common topic of discussion in the trauma-informed support group she runs for teens. Poverty,

Stress over money is common among teens, but learning about personal finance can help reduce that stress.

she has found, can cause traumas that "lead into phases of PTSD [post-traumatic stress disorder], where you see kids grow up to either have severely detached relationships with money or severely insufficient or maladaptive relationships with money."[3]

Personal Finance Education

Learning about personal finances is the key to making wise financial decisions, but many teens aren't being taught these skills. Increased knowledge about personal finance, such as how to budget and plan for their financial futures, can increase confidence in handling personal finances and reduce worry and stress. This is why half of the states in the United States are now requiring personal finance courses as part of their curricula. For example, starting in 2027 all students attending public and charter high schools in California will have to take a semester of a financial literacy course. And California students agree that taking a financial literacy course might actually be more useful than other required courses such as physical education. Saron Muluneh, a senior at a San Diego high school, believes that courses like this would have helped her manage the stipend she got from a recent internship. She says, "I need to know how to manage all that, honestly. Because I do not want to blow through all of that. Like, I can use that money towards college, towards myself, towards buying a new car."[4] She also wants to be able to navigate the tricky parts of personal finance, such as learning about how to avoid scammers, how to invest and get insurance, and even how she might pay for a house of her own in the future.

Learning about personal finance basics gives teens the tools to make good financial decisions now and in adulthood. This helps them avoid common mistakes such as overspending, taking on unnecessary credit card debt, and not saving for the future. It also helps manage stress resulting from money worries and avoid financial mistakes with long-term consequences that can have an impact on their mental health.

CHAPTER ONE

How to Budget

Gen Z is the first generation to have lived their entire preteen and teen years with social media access. And for young people like twenty-three-year-old Jacey Insani, being on social media has even impacted how she spends money. "I do think that within our generation," she reflects, "social media has contributed to over-consumerism and others feeling pressured to buy the nicest and newest things to keep up with trends and popular items."[5]

The urge to be able to imitate the influencers that dominate platforms like TikTok and Instagram by purchasing the clothing, accessories, and makeup they wear is strong. Using "buy now, pay later" services such as Afterpay and Klarna also makes it tempting to purchase items without having the money to pay for them now. Insani has learned from using these services in the past, saying, "I love shopping with my friends, and it's really enticing seeing that something is going to cost cheaper in the moment, but it's not worth the anxiety I have to pay that money back."[6]

Overspending

Overspending among teens and young adults is common. While lack of knowledge about personal finance is a contributing factor, so is the desire to spend money on things such as clothing that will help them follow trends and fit in with peers. Not having the money to spend on these items can leave teens feeling left out or isolated. Teens who are given spending money, rather than earning it, can also struggle with overspending, especially if there are no boundaries or limits on what they spend.

> "I do think that within our generation social media has contributed to over-consumerism and others feeling pressured to buy the nicest and newest things to keep up with trends and popular items."[5]
>
> —Jacey Insani, twenty-three-year-old former overspender

While the influence of friends can be strong, so can that of social media influencers and social media advertisements. When adult members of Gen Z, those aged eighteen to twenty-seven, were polled in 2024 by the online loan service LendingTree, 65 percent said that they had felt pressured by social media to buy something that they didn't need. Teens, in particular, represent a rich market for many companies. These companies target them with ads on social media sites so that they can tap into teen spending power. A 2022 study by the Harvard T.H. Chan School of Public Health found that combined Facebook, Instagram, Snapchat, TikTok, X, and YouTube advertisement revenue from American teens under age eighteen was almost $11 billion. The ease of buying products and services online also encourages impulsive buying, further simplified by "buy-now-pay-later" services that encourage teens to purchase items that they don't have the money to buy. Truth in Advertising, a nonprofit focusing on false and deceptive advertising, identifies teens as being particularly vulnerable to social media advertising, saying:

> [Teens] follow the "likes." This behavior is partly due to the fact that critical reasoning and decision-making abilities are not fully developed until the mid-to-late 20s. . . . As they are exposed to more products through social media, either through sponsored ads or brand influencers, the pressure to belong can be a strong motivator to purchase. Teens are more prone to impulse buying, and may be more inclined to make a sudden purchase to fit in.[7]

What Is a Budget?

College sophomore Karla Hernandez found that most of her overspending occurred during her first year of college when her mother was providing her with a monthly allowance and extra money whenever she blew through the allowance. She bought whatever she needed or wanted without really thinking about how much anything cost. That changed in her second semester in college, when her parents stopped providing a monthly allowance. "I came to the realization: OK, I need to spend my money wisely." she says, "Knowing that I have $100 in my account doesn't mean I need to spend it all. I could put some into my savings and some of it for emergency, for when I really need it."[8]

But how do you keep track of the money you have and the money you spend? And how do you avoid overspending? The answer is to create a budget. Erin Gobler is a money coach. She helps her clients create budgets and make better choices with

A girl films herself unboxing her online purchase. Social media influences teen spending, often making them feel pressured to buy things that they cannot afford.

> "Budgeting is one of the most important things you can do to take control of your finances and improve your future."[9]
>
> —Erin Gobler, money coach

their money. She says many of her adult clients express regret that they didn't start using a budget earlier. This is one reason she recommends that teens learn about and start using a budget before they reach adulthood. "Budgeting is one of the most important things you can do to take control of your finances and improve your future," she says. "Most people don't start budgeting until far later [in] life and aren't convinced to start until they've hit financial roadblocks."[9] Creating a budget might seem overwhelming, but it really is just a plan to determine how much money you have coming in and how much will be going out during a month or pay period or even a year.

Creating a budget begins with determining how much money you have coming in every month: your income. This can include money you earn from a part-time job, gifts, and allowance. You might determine that your income every month is from the two five-hour shifts you work a week, resulting in an after-tax income of $480 in a typical month. After determining income, you'll write down all the things you spend money on each month: your expenses. If you have records such as bank statements or receipts, these can be helpful to remember what you have been spending your money on, but if not, just write down what you remember and fill in any gaps later. A fixed expense is an expense that is the same every month, which can include items like car insurance, loan payments, and subscriptions. Other expenses—such as clothing, eating out, entertainment, gas, and gifts—might vary, but based on both past spending and how much money you have available to spend, you can eventually determine a good amount to budget for those categories as well.

Different Budgeting Methods

There is no one-size-fits-all budget, but there are well-established budgeting methods that can work for most anyone. The budget method frequently recommended by personal finance experts is the 50/30/20 budget. This budget is set up by allocating your

In-App Purchases Can Blow Your Budget

Children, teens, and adults are spending hundreds and even thousands of dollars in an unusual place: the world of apps. The purchases don't result in any tangible items but rather virtual upgrades, prizes, and coins in games such as Roblox. In-app purchases both lend themselves to impulsive buying and blur the line between real and pretend money, which can make them especially tempting and dangerous for teens. Jessica Johnson was shocked when she realized that her preteen son had spent $16,293.10 on in-app purchases. "It's intentionally designed to be a brain chemistry experience that one would get as an adult in a casino," Johnson says. "It's creating a compulsion to want to keep going. I think that's what drove my son to keep pushing the button, get more players, to run faster." This compulsion can quickly turn into overspending to the tune of hundreds or even thousands of dollars. Teens who want to curb in-app spending should remove credit or debit cards connected to their accounts, switch off in-app spending, or set a budget amount for in-app spending and then keep track of purchases.

Quoted in Nicole Pelletiere, "Mom Warns Parents After Son Charges $16K on In-App Game Purchases," *Good Morning America*, December 18, 2022. www.goodmorningamerica.com.

income into percentages: 50 percent of your money should go toward the things that you need, 30 percent to things that you want, and 20 percent to savings. Here's an example of what this type of budget might look like for a teen who earns $480 a month from their part-time job. They would first allot 50 percent of that income, which would be $240, for needs or items that must be paid every month, such as car insurance, gas, and cell phone service. Thirty percent, or $144, of this teen's budget would be for wants, which could include clothing, subscriptions, hobby purchases, eating out, and entertainment. This is the category that has the most flexibility. If you are looking to go shopping for back-to-school clothing in August, you might dedicate your entire wants budget for the month for that, putting off going to the movies or fast-food runs. The final 20 percent of the budget, $96, should be dedicated to savings goals.

This budget method can be a good reminder that items in the needs column get priority, meaning you might have to rethink your spending in the wants categories. While this budget method can work for many people, it doesn't allow for much flexibility due to the set percentages dedicated to needs, wants, and savings.

Another common budgeting method is the zero-based budget, which accounts for every single dollar you receive in income. This might seem overwhelming, but really it's just based on the fact that if you don't determine a destination for all your money (or what you will spend or save it for), you are more likely to spend it more impulsively. This is a good budget for someone who does not have a steady monthly income. Each month, you simply begin with your income and then subtract expenses, starting with essentials and savings until you've got nothing left. For example, one month a teen might earn $250 by babysitting, be gifted $50 for their birthday, and earn $25 from selling clothing, resulting in $325 of total income for the month. They first allot $75 for a public transport pass (a monthly need), then $100 for savings, and then a set amount budgeted for food, entertainment, or other wants. Unplanned income, such as that $50 birthday gift, could be spent on wants or put directly into savings. This budget can be more

Part of creating a budget is writing down all of your expenses, which are the things you spend money on each month.

How Teens Spend Their Money

Budgets are one of the best tools for keeping spending for wants under control. And according to a new survey, teens have a lot of wants. Thousands of American teens took part in the Spring 2025 Taking Stock with Teens survey conducted by the investment bank and financial services company, Piper Sandler. The survey found that teens spent on average $2,388 a year, largely on clothing, makeup and skin care, food, and entertainment. These types of purchases offer a way for teens to express themselves, try out new trends, and either fit in with or stand out from their peers. Entertainment options such as phones, video games, concerts, and meals at restaurants are popular ways for teens to connect with friends. Although these may seem like needs, they are usually placed in the category of wants. Subscriptions, purchases for hobbies, activities with friends, books, memberships, and new tech tools are other wants that teens spend money on. The key to not letting all these types of purchases get out of control is to evaluate your wants each month, budget for the ones that matter most, and save the others for another date.

labor intensive, because it relies on creating a new budget every month and closely tracking expenses.

Another budget method that can be helpful for teens just learning to budget is the cash envelope system, which is often used in combination with another budgeting method. This method literally involves putting a set amount of cash into different envelopes each month and keeping it in a safe place in your house or apartment. The idea is to withdraw cash amounts as needed each month to cover categories that are variable or don't cost the same set amount every month, like eating out, hobbies, gas, or hair and skin care. Expenses that are a set amount every month and savings are still paid out in the usual way, whether by automatic electronic payments or cash. While this method might seem old-fashioned, it has actually become popular with influencers on TikTok and other social media sites. The thinking behind this cash-only budgeting method is that impulse-buying is a lot easier when using credit cards, debit cards, and payment apps than if you have to fork over the actual cash. The act of paying with cash helps individuals think more about what they are buying before they spend the money. This, in turn, can reduce overspending. For variable expenses, a budget for each category is determined, and cash in that amount is put in an envelope for that month; once the money is gone, there is no more for the month.

While the cash envelope system can be a good way to reduce impulsive spending and also help you consider whether you really need or want an item, it can be time consuming at the beginning of each month. There is also a risk of the cash being lost or stolen, so where you keep the envelopes and how much you carry with you should be considered. Digital payments and online purchases also are more challenging with this system. However, some budget apps are now offering digital wallets, which allow you to use a similar budgeting mindset to place digital cash in envelopes for the month.

Track Your Spending

An important part of budgeting is tracking what you spend over the course of a month. Tracking can be done with a spreadsheet or with a budgeting app. Many banks also offer features that allow

One common budgeting method is the zero-based budget, which accounts for every single dollar you receive, including a set amount budgeted for things like food and entertainment.

account holders to track spending and create a budget. Tracking monthly expenses can show you how close you are to meeting your budget goals, where you fall short, and where to make adjustments.

Often, overspending results in your not having the money to pay for needs later in the month. One way to have more money to pay for the things that you want is to increase your income. Another is to decrease your expenses. If, for example, you want to go to two concerts this month, to stay within your budget, you might have to put off buying the new outfit you've been looking at for at least another month. Or you could decide to cancel a streaming subscription or cook dinner at home a couple of nights instead of going out to restaurants. Underspending—or having money left over once your needs, wants, and savings goals are taken care of for the month—is less likely, but it could happen. It's good to have a plan for that money if it ever occurs. You want to think about whether this money will go directly into savings or be rolled into a budget category for the next month.

It is important to remember that it is easy to make mistakes when you're learning something new. Budgeting takes practice. So don't beat yourself up if you go over budget one month. According to personal finance app Credit Karma, "Mistakes happen, but what's important is what you learn from them. Did you fall short of your savings goal and now have to skip a fun activity or settle for a cheaper alternative? Reflect on why that happened, and think about how to improve next time. Good spending and saving habits come with practice."[10] Even if everything is going as planned, budgeting requires some flexibility. Income will change based on pay and frequency of a job or side gigs and whether it's the school year or summer break. Expenses can also change and increase as you get older.

"Mistakes happen, but what's important is what you learn from them. . . . Good spending and saving habits come with practice."[10]

—Credit Karma, personal finance app

CHAPTER TWO

How to Save Money

When Ashley Eli turned sixteen, she got her first part-time job at McDonald's and took a second job working for Best Buy. Unlike many teens her age, she had a plan for how she wanted to use her earnings. She wanted to buy a car. To do that, she set a goal for herself. She would save a portion of her earnings for one full year. "If you're working a lot like I was take 100 out of your paycheck and use that for the month . . . save the rest, don't touch the rest,"[11] Eli advises. Between her savings and money borrowed from her parents (which she is paying back), Eli was able to buy a car. She went with a used car—a basic model that would get her where she needs to go—to keep the expense down.

Savings Goals

Eli's purchase of a car could be considered a long-term savings goal. She determined that she wanted to purchase a car, set a goal of how much money she wanted to save, and then found two part-time jobs to earn the money. After a year, she took her savings, along with some money from her parents, and purchased a car. Other long-term savings goals may include saving for an apartment security deposit and first month's rent, college expenses, or a postgraduation trip. Long-term goals are for items or experiences that are at least a year away or that will require you to save up for about that long. Whatever you're saving for, determining a long-term goal in advance will give you the time you need to save enough money.

> "Take the time to determine what you can afford to save so that we're not putting money into savings just to take it right back."[12]
>
> —Raya Reaves, finance coach

Short-term goals are ones that you will need the money for in the near future, perhaps in a few months' time. One such goal could be setting aside a predetermined amount of money every month for Christmas gifts, so money spent on gifts doesn't have to come out of only your December budget. Other short-term goals could be saving for spending money on an upcoming family vacation, a pricey concert ticket, a prom dress, or items for hobbies such as a new guitar or snowboard.

Whatever your savings goals might be, it is important to remember that while saving should be a priority, paying for essentials comes first. The amount you save for short-term or long-term goals should be determined accordingly. Finance coach Raya Reaves has seen budgeting too much for savings result in the bad habit of taking from savings for everyday expenses regularly. "A lot of times I see people wanting to be aggressive with their savings goals . . . but when we look at their budget, that money was needed to make sure they have grocery money,"

By budgeting the money earned from a part-time job, teens can work toward achieving a long-term savings goal.

Savings Accounts for Teens

While some bank accounts are for adults only, there are also savings accounts that have been created with features just for teens. Some of best features of these accounts are no or low minimum deposits, no minimum balance requirements, and no maintenance fees. That means that teens can start their accounts with whatever amount they have and don't have to worry about keeping a certain amount in their accounts to avoid penalties or pay other fees to keep the account open. Some of these accounts also include a debit card, which allows teens to make card-based purchases online and in person without having to have a checking account. The top teen savings accounts, according to *Forbes*, include Capital One and FourLeaf Federal Credit Union. A Capital One Kids Savings account has a higher annual percentage yield (APY) than many other teen savings accounts, and it can be kept into adulthood without having to switch to another account. FourLeaf Federal Credit Union Student Savings is similar in that it offers a high APY, digital banking, and conversion to an adult savings account.

says Reaves. "Take the time to determine what you can afford to save so that we're not putting money into savings just to take it right back."[12]

Where to Save Your Money

Most Americans keep their savings in traditional bank savings accounts. Opening this type of account typically requires a small first deposit—sometimes as little as five dollars. Even if you regularly add money to the account—from a part-time job or birthday gifts of money, for instance—you probably won't earn any (or much) interest on your savings. For non-teens, they may have fees and restrictions such as limits on how many withdrawals you can make per month or a minimum amount you must keep in the account to avoid being charged fees. Traditional savings accounts are mostly a safe place to keep your money until you need to spend it.

However, if you keep your money in an account that doesn't earn interest or keep taking money out of the account, then you can miss out on the power of compound interest over time. Compound interest is when your money earns interest on both the money you put into the account and on the interest earned on that money. Most traditional banks, online banks, and credit unions do offer interest rate accounts, meaning accounts that pay interest on the money you save. Some of these offer relatively high-interest accounts, often with no fees and low initial deposits. These are known as high-yield savings accounts. According to *Forbes*, in 2025 these accounts offered as high as 4.30 percent annual percentage yield (APY). APY is the amount of interest that the account will earn in a year. An obvious drawback for online banks is that they do not offer physical locations for banking, which can make cash deposits and withdrawals challenging. However, some online banks now offer deposits and withdrawals at ATMs and stores through a checking account connected to a savings account.

If one or more of your savings goals is long term and you will not need to access the money for that time frame, a certificate of deposit (CD) is another account option. These accounts have a fixed APY for a set number of months, while both traditional and high-yield savings accounts have changeable interest rates. CDs with a traditional or online bank generally range from a six-month to sixty-month term. With a preset APY, you will know exactly how much your deposit will earn over the term you choose. For example, an initial deposit of $1,000 at a 3.5 percent APY will earn $71.23 in interest on a 24-month CD. Early withdrawals can be made from CDs, but they generally incur penalties, so it's best to only put in money that won't be needed right away. A CD should also never be your only savings account, since more money cannot be deposited over the course of the term either.

How to Save Money Effectively

If you would like to increase the amount of money you are saving to reach savings goals quicker, you have two options: reduce your expenses or increase your income. Or you can really go all in and do both. The cash envelope budget system can be one way to reduce spending, especially for budget categories that are wants

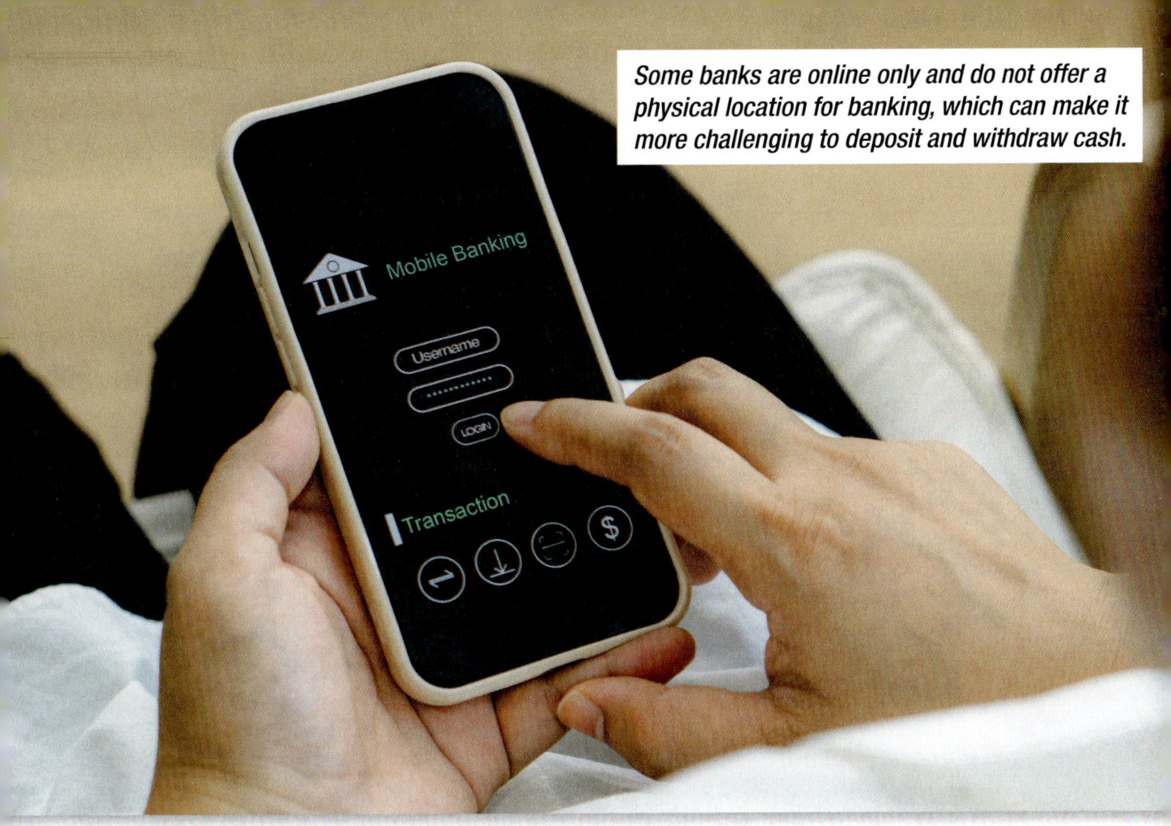

Some banks are online only and do not offer a physical location for banking, which can make it more challenging to deposit and withdraw cash.

rather than needs. "Studies have found that when someone is using cash rather than a debit or credit card, they actually spend about 9% less at checkout because they're more conscientious about the prices and limitations, whereas using a credit card often feels like unlimited money,"[13] says Lauren Anastasio, director of financial advice at Stash, a banking and investment platform.

At fourteen, bored during the early days of the pandemic, Paula began to explore ways she could earn money online. She tried different side hustles, including taking surveys on survey apps, starting her own YouTube channels, and selling clothing on Poshmark. At first she was spending all of the money she earned right away. But then she realized that she also wanted to save some money for the future. She motivated herself by getting specific, knowing what she was saving for and why. "Having a strong why is absolutely essential to achieving your goals, to achieving your money goals," Paula says. "You will have times where you are put under pressure. You will have times where you want to spend all your money and having a strong why will help you build

> "Having a strong why is absolutely essential to achieving your goals, to achieving your money goals. . . . You will have times where you want to spend all your money and having a strong why will help you build discipline."[14]
>
> —Paula, teen with savings goals

discipline."[14] A great way to remember your why is by creating a vision board that includes pictures of what you are saving for or making it your phone background. Having a constant reminder of the item or experience you are saving for can be great motivation to spend less and save more.

Being around friends who have more money to spend than you do can be extra challenging. Sometimes it helps just to talk with those friends about lower-cost or no-cost activities that you can do together. Or share your savings goals with a friend or two and you might find they have similar goals. Anastasio says:

> If you are saving up for prom or spring break, sharing that with a friend can be really motivating because you'll have the power of two looking for opportunities to save.

Side Gigs to Increase Savings

A part-time job with regular hours is a great way to earn money for the things you want and need, especially during the summer. Side gigs can also provide an extra boost for your savings and help you accomplish your savings goals more quickly. Here are some common teen side gigs:

- House or pet sitting
- Babysitting or tutoring
- Offering art or music lessons
- Mowing lawns, gardening, dog walking, or cleaning for neighbors
- Selling artistic creations at craft fairs or on Etsy
- Thrifting and reselling clothing and other items
- Earning gift cards by taking surveys and joining focus groups
- Washing and detailing cars
- Repairing bikes, computers, and so on
- Writing and graphic design

By putting money in a savings account every month, teens can make a bigger purchase, like a car, a reality.

They might offer to watch a movie at one of your houses instead of going to the movie theater. They'll be someone else to hold you accountable and cheer you on when you need some help.[15]

Why Start Saving Now?

A common question surrounding saving is whether it is necessary to start saving as a teen. The answer is, yes, it is a good idea to learn how to save money early—before the responsibilities of adulthood kick in. Studies show that individuals who start saving as teens are more likely to continue to do so as adults. Setting money aside for emergencies and for things that you'd like to purchase in the future is important because then you don't have to go into debt to afford the things that you need and want or go without them. It's something that many adults struggle to put into practice. In a 2024 *Forbes* survey on saving habits, 28 percent of the adult respondents said they had less than $1,000 in savings. An emergency room visit, a car needing repairs, or a loss of income can quickly eliminate those savings. This is why financial experts recommend that adults have an emergency account with a minimum of $1,000, preferably more, to cover surprise expenses or in the case of job loss.

The same survey found that Gen Z respondents were the most likely to dig into their savings for daily and weekly regular expenses. If you are budgeting wisely, you shouldn't need to use money that you have in savings for this purpose. Every time you take money out, reaching the savings goal you have will take even longer. *Forbes* states, "Ideally, the money in your savings account should be reserved for unexpected expenses or a specific item you've been saving for. While it's not the end of the world if you dip into your savings for daily expenses like grocery bills or shopping sprees, this can stunt the growth of your savings."[16]

> **"Ideally, the money in your savings account should be reserved for unexpected expenses or a specific item you've been saving for."[16]**
>
> —*Forbes*, a business and finance magazine

Saving for future expenses or desired purchases is the key to setting and achieving financial goals for the future. While every teen's saving goals might look a little different, prioritizing setting aside money every month into savings can help make their desired purchases a reality. Saving also helps form the habits needed to save for larger purchases and longer-term goals in adulthood, such as an emergency fund, house down payment, or savings for retirement.

CHAPTER THREE

How to Invest and Grow Your Money

Jack Rosenthal got started early with investing. He began investing at age eight, after his grandfather opened a custodial account for him. This type of account allows a child or teen to have an investment account in their name under the supervision of an adult. Initially, his grandfather decided what stocks to invest in, but eventually Rosenthal became actively involved. "I'd send him emails—buy this, sell that,"[17] says Rosenthal. At fifteen he started a high school investment club. This club was a little different from most other teen investment clubs. Instead of using imaginary money to learn about investing, the members of Rosenthal's club were investing real money in real companies. Each club member invested $1,000 in a real investment account. The club began with twenty members. It had grown to one hundred by the time Rosenthal graduated, and the investment account was worth $120,000. The process had an added benefit for Rosenthal: He had learned enough about investing to write a book that he called *Teen Investing*. In it he describes the basics of investing. His book defines relevant terminology, explains how and where to invest, and describes the factors he considers when making his own investment decisions.

Many teens don't have $1,000 to invest, but that doesn't mean that they are too young to learn about investing or can't start investing with a much smaller amount. Sophia Castiblanco, a teen who invested her way to her own new car,

"I think it's important to realize that even if you just invest like $20 a month, or I mean a super small amount, you can still grow that over time."[18]

—Sophia Castiblanco, a teen investor

notes that many people have misconceptions about investing. "There's no minimum age to start," Castiblanco says. "I think it's important to realize that even if you just invest like $20 a month, or I mean a super small amount, you can still grow that over time."[18]

Why Teens Aren't Investing

Knowledge about investing has increased among the teen population due to personal finance courses in schools and social media posts with investing tips by both financial experts and young investors. Social media posts have made the process more appealing by explaining the investment process in simpler terms and raising awareness that investing is not just reserved for adults. Financial services companies also have recognized the need for more tools, accounts, and apps that help teens learn about investing and be able to invest themselves. Charles Schwab, a financial services company that offers custodial accounts for chil-

Some teens have the opportunity to learn about investing by taking a personal finance course in school.

Should You Invest in Crypto?

Cryptocurrency is all the rage, but what is it exactly? Unlike paper currency, crypto is a form of payment that exists only in digital form. It is stored in a digital wallet, with security features that allow it to be accessed with a private key. The appeal of crypto is partially that it has performed better than other investments such as stocks. Bitcoin, a type of cryptocurrency, has increased in value from less than 1 cent to $100,000 from 2009 to 2025. It also appeals to those with an interest in technology innovation, since it utilizes blockchain, a tamper-resistant digital system that tracks crypto transactions.

Investing in cryptocurrency is not without risks, however. Cryptocurrency prices can change rapidly and there are generally fees for every transaction. As a result, some investors have made a lot of money, while others have lost money. Another criticism that cryptocurrency has received is that, like artificial intelligence, crypto creation and transactions consume massive amounts of energy. A January 2025 Statista report found that one Bitcoin transaction used the same amount of energy as hundreds of thousands of Visa credit card transactions.

dren and teens, saw a jump in these accounts from 120,000 in 2019 to over 300,000 in 2023. Fidelity's 2023 Teens and Money Study found that 23 percent of the teen respondents were already investing, and 90 percent saw investing as a way to save for the future.

Kelly Lannan, a senior vice president at Fidelity, says that the company's study also revealed some of the reasons that teens aren't investing. "Of the teens that are saying they're not investing, 31% are saying they think they're too young, and 20% they're saying they don't have enough money to invest," Lannan says. "[This is] creating a little bit of a barrier between actually those who are getting started and who's not."[19] Investing can also feel overwhelming to many teens, who may feel that they don't have the finance or stock market knowledge to make good decisions and that it is too complicated to learn. Fear of losing money that they have invested and being worse off than when they began can also be a reason to choose to put money into a location that feels more secure, such as a savings account.

Often, family values and experiences around money can influence how teens feel about trying to invest and their general confidence surrounding personal finances. Many adults also have knowledge gaps or don't feel confident investing, even if they do want their children to learn. "In every study we did, parents would be like, 'Yeah, I want my kid to learn about investing . . .' and then off to the side, they're like, 'Can you teach me too?'" says Lannan. "There's such a desire by parents to make sure their kids are educated, but at the same time, they want to be educated as well."[20]

Defining Investing Terminology

One of the challenging things about investing is all of the terminology. When people talk about investing, they use terms like *stocks*, *bonds*, and *shares*. Listening to conversations about investing can feel like people are speaking a foreign language that you don't understand. Teens who want to know more about investing can start by learning what these terms mean.

Stocks represent part ownership of a publicly traded company. Any member of the public has the opportunity to invest money in that company by purchasing shares, which are units of the company's stock. Buying shares makes you a shareholder—technically, a part owner of that company.

The stock market is the network of all the places where buying and selling of shares occurs, which is known as trading. Often, when someone refers to the stock market or stock exchange, they are speaking of the New York Stock Exchange, which is the largest in the world. The S&P 500 is the public reporting of the share prices of the top five hundred companies in the New York Stock Exchange. Share prices can be impacted by a number of factors, from the health of the company itself, to inflation, unemployment, governmental actions, national or global unrest, and natural disasters.

An alternative to stocks, which have share prices that go up and down with the market, are bonds. Bonds are essentially lending money to a company or organization in exchange for interest

Asset allocation is the concept of spreading investments across different types of assets, with the ideal allocation based on risk tolerance.

on the original amount you invested. Bonds can be issued by both private and public companies, as well as state, regional, and the federal government. Interest is paid regularly, and once the bond matures (or the bond term is completed, which could be one to thirty years, depending on the bond terms), you receive the original investment amount back. While there is less risk involved in investing in bonds, the returns, or money you earn above what you originally invested, is generally less than that of stocks.

Investing in mutual funds or exchange-traded funds (ETFs) is a good way to spread out risk. A mutual fund is a group of stocks, bonds, and other investments that is managed by a professional. Instead of purchasing and selling shares yourself, the mutual fund makes these trades once a day based on the market. An ETF is similar in that it is a group of investments but has lower initial investments and can be traded multiple times a day, just like stocks.

When you begin trading on the stock market, there are some additional terms to understand. Your risk tolerance is how much risk you are willing to take at any given point with your investments. Riskier investments may end up benefiting you, or they could result in losing money. Risk tolerance is based on several factors, including your age and investment goals. For example,

What About Retirement?

Retirement may seem way, way off in the future now, but it is important to at least understand the options as a teen so you can start saving for your future as early as possible. Accounts that are specifically earmarked for retirement can help you reduce the amount of income taxes you pay (once you have a steady income) and take advantage of the power of compound interest.

Regular IRA: Anyone with earned income can open an IRA account. The money deposited into an IRA account is not subject to income taxes, but you will owe taxes once you start withdrawing money from the account.

Roth IRA: Unlike a regular IRA, deposits to a Roth IRA are taxed up front rather than when the money is withdrawn. This type of retirement account is often recommended for teens and young people, since earnings (and thus income taxes) tend to be lower at the start of a career than at the end.

401(k): These are employer-sponsored accounts that let you put part of your paycheck in the account before taxes. Some employers may also match your contribution up to a certain percentage of your salary.

an individual nearing retirement or with a lower income likely will be a conservative investor, while a younger individual or one with more money to invest could choose a more aggressive investment strategy. A younger investor has more time to wait out fluctuations in the stock market, while an individual who is near retirement or already retired could end up losing money that they likely will not recover in time to spend on living expenses.

Asset allocation is how your investments are spread across the different types of assets. The ideal asset allocation for each person is largely based on their risk tolerance. Diversification means that your investments are diverse, so they are in different stocks, bonds, and other investments. Teen Rachael Kim learned the importance of diversification during her early investing when she traded shares of one company, AMC Entertainment Holdings. Although she made a 300 percent return on her investment, Kim says she began to question whether her gains were sustainable. "For a little while, I got addicted to that adrenaline," Kim says. "But as I began researching more, I realized it was highly unlikely to continue that aggressive profit."[21]

Investing Strategies

You may have heard the expression "Don't put all your eggs in one basket." This is especially true while investing. Having a variety of stocks, bonds, and other investments is the best way to spread out your risk so you don't end up losing a great deal of money. The simplest way to achieve this is by investing in funds that are already diversified or include a variety of different companies and investments. If researching and monitoring your investments is something that doesn't appeal to you, the ability to purchase shares in a fund and have it managed by someone else is an option as well.

It can be difficult to predict the ups and downs of share prices in the stock market, so another recommended strategy is "Buy and hold," which means buying stocks and holding on to them for a longer term, no matter what happens with the market. How volatile the stock market can be was hard to stomach for thirteen-year-old Kaida Benes at first, who was using money saved from doing chores to invest in a financial learning app. Benes says she's learned over time that "stocks go up and down. It's fine, it just happens."[22]

> "Stocks go up and down. It's fine, it just happens."[22]
>
> —Kaida Benes, thirteen-year-old investor

Sticking it out in the stock market is important, because over the longer term there is the potential to earn more than you could earn even in a high yield savings account. Over the past thirty years, the S&P 500 index has had an annualized total return of 10 percent, which means that investments have earned the equivalent of a savings account with a 10 percent APY. And that compound interest will work its magic just like it does in a savings account. Starting to contribute $150 a month into an investment account at age seventeen could turn into over $1 million if you retire at age sixty-five and have an average return of 8 percent. "It's understandably exciting to imagine, say, $150 turning into a million dollars," says Melanie Mortimer, president of the SIFMA Foundation, which works to educate kids and teens about the stock market. "Even though that takes time, if you recognize the impact of compound interest, it'll feed into appreciation for the long-term retirement conversation."[23]

Retirement accounts are actually the investment accounts of choice for most Americans, since in non-retirement investment accounts, both the money you put in and the money you earn are subject to income tax. Retirement accounts allow the investor to not have to pay as much in income tax. Investopedia, an online investing site, believes that teens are ideal candidates for a Roth individual retirement account (or IRA). Roth IRA accounts are funded with after-tax money. Teens who have part-time or summer jobs or who earn money from their own business endeavors are well placed to start a Roth IRA. "Since most teens do not earn enough to pay federal income taxes—or are in the lowest bracket—the Roth IRA's 'pay taxes now, grow tax-free later' model becomes incredibly efficient,"[24] Investopedia reports.

How to Get Started Investing

Teens who are under eighteen usually need a family member to open a custodial account, which means that the adult opens and manages the account until the teen is eighteen or twenty-one, depending on their state of residency. Many financial services companies have developed teen-centric accounts that include educational investing tools and apps. Most custodial accounts require that the parent or guardian have their own account with the brokerage firm. Beyond the adult being responsible for opening the account, a custodial account also allows them to monitor account activity, set alerts, and make deposits into the account. For teens who are interested in learning about investing, a custodial account offers the opportunity to buy and sell stocks while

A teen under age eighteen who wants to open an investment account will usually need to do so with a family member.

still having the supervision and input of an adult in their life. Other benefits of the custodial accounts offered by many companies include no fees, no account minimums, and the option to start investing with as little as just one dollar.

Beyond traditional custodial accounts, financial learning apps such as Greenlight were developed to teach teens about investing. The app offers games that teach the basics of personal finance. It also includes tools for researching stocks and ETFs.

For teens who don't want to get into the nitty-gritty of stock trading and choosing what to invest in, some custodial accounts automatically put deposits into a predetermined aggressive portfolio. One such company, Acorn Early Invest, also has the unique benefit of a 1 percent match, which means that Acorn Early will add 1 percent of what you contribute into your account. If you prefer not to take the approach of having a portfolio chosen for you, once an account is set up, it is time to research the stocks, ETFs, and mutual funds you may be interested in investing in.

"If your friend says a stock is great, don't immediately buy or sell based on their word alone. The market always has ups and downs, but you want to build that investment value over time and benefit from compounding interest."[25]

—Melanie Mortimer, president of the SIFMA Foundation

What are the stores you shop at, the companies that you and your friends are purchasing products from? This may be a good place to start. However, Mortimer warns, "If your friend says a stock is great, don't immediately buy or sell based on their word alone. The market always has ups and downs, but you want to build that investment value over time and benefit from compounding interest."[25]

Investing club founder Rosenthal also recommends finding companies that are likely to be around for a long time. Rosenthal says, "Think of the stocks that will exist 20 or 30 years from now, and chances are those stocks will do very well over your lifetime."[26]

With a lot of new terminology and concepts to understand, investing can sometimes feel overwhelming and confusing. However, the teen years are an ideal time to learn the basics before investing large amounts of money. Starting to invest small amounts of money now will not only build investing habits and foundational investment knowledge but also help you start investing in your financial future.

CHAPTER FOUR

All About Credit and Debt

Malik Peay has graduated from college, but one of his first financial choices before he began was to get a credit card. He planned to use it for necessities like groceries, but he ended up putting other expenses on the card that he wasn't able to pay off every month. "I thought it was a smart idea for myself because I wanted to fit in with my wealthier peers. I wanted the full college experience. But I wish I had educated myself more on credit card interest rates and monthly payments,"[27] Peay says. He still has several thousand dollars of credit card debt to pay off, which he is prioritizing by taking on extra work.

Peay's story is not unusual. Many Americans depend on credit cards—both for necessities and for the extras that make life easier and more enjoyable. And more teens are getting access to credit cards, often without understanding how they work or learning about best practices. A 2024 LendingTree study found that 59 percent of respondents had given their credit or debit card to their child to use, and a CreditCards.com poll found that 6 million parent respondents had a teen under eighteen with their own credit card.

> "I wish I had educated myself more on credit card interest rates and monthly payments."[27]
>
> —Malik Peay, college graduate

How Credit Cards Work

To avoid problems later, experts say it's important for teens to learn how credit cards work, and the potential risks they pose, before obtaining a credit card. A credit card can be swiped, inserted, or tapped for in-person payments or have its information inputted for online purchases. However, instead of drawing from an existing bank account, as happens with a debit card, payments put on a credit card are loans. Like any loan, they have to be paid back to the lender, meaning the credit card company or bank. A credit card has a credit limit, or a maximum amount of money that you can be lent. All purchases are put against this limit. It is best practice and best for your wallet if you pay off your credit card balance (the amount of money you owe to the credit card company) in full every month, but all credit cards have a set minimum payment amount that you must pay or you will incur late payment fees.

Any unpaid balance going forward will be charged interest. The interest amount is either variable, which means it can change over time, or fixed, which doesn't change. Either way, credit card interest—known as an annual percentage rate (APR)—is usually high. According to *Forbes*, in 2025 the average APR for credit card accounts was 21.91 percent. This means over the course of a year, a credit card balance of $1,000 will have increased to $1,219.10. And if penalty fees and additional purchases are added to a credit card balance, it can increase further. Only making minimum payments can make it hard to make a dent in debt that keeps growing and can quickly become overwhelming.

Ballooning Debt

Building up debt is easy. Paying off debt can be difficult, especially when that debt is spread across multiple credit cards. Lauren Pellegrino, now twenty-five, got her first credit card at eighteen and quickly saw her debt balloon. She reflects, "I . . . opened up a $500 Capital One credit card to help build credit and learn how to responsibly use it. . . . [I had a] $2,000–$3,000 credit limit across three different cards because I kept getting credit card offers and credit limit increases. . . . Once interest started accruing, the debt just spiraled out of control and became impossible to keep up with."[28] Now with $9,000 of debt to pay off, she feels less hope-

Some teens are getting access to credit cards without understanding how they work, and this can quickly lead to a large amount of debt.

ful about going to college. Taking out student loans on top of her existing debt just isn't an option.

But credit card debt isn't inevitable. Used wisely, a credit card can be a useful tool. "Credit cards don't have to be scary or dangerous." says Hannah Oh, a shopping editor at *Cosmopolitan*, "You'll avoid scary debt by remembering that your credit card isn't free money—so you should only spend what you can pay off right away."[29]

Teens under eighteen can't obtain a credit card in their own name, but they can become an authorized user with their own card on their parent's or guardian's account. This is a good way to both have your credit card usage monitored and start building your credit without the risks and responsibility of your own credit card account. At eighteen, there are more options

"You'll avoid scary debt by remembering that your credit card isn't free money—so you should only spend what you can pay off right away."[29]

—Hannah Oh, shopping editor at *Cosmopolitan*

Smart Ways to Build Credit

You don't need to go into thousands of dollars debt or max out your credit card limit to have a credit score. Here are some smart ways to build credit as a teen.

Acquire your own cell phone account. Phone and other utility bills in your name (and rent) are often reported to the credit bureaus. If not, you can utilize a service that will report these accounts to credit bureaus.

Whether it is a credit card, cell phone bill, or rent, on-time payment is critical to maintaining a good credit score. Make sure all these bills are accounted for in your budget and ideally are paid out of your account automatically.

Don't go on a shopping spree with your shiny new credit card. Experts recommend only having 30 percent or less of your credit limit as your credit card balance at any given time. So, if your credit limit is $1,500, your credit card balance should ideally be $450 or less.

available, but the credit card application process can often be more challenging for those without an income or prior credit history. For those individuals a good beginning option is a secured credit card, says Vivian Tu, the chief executive officer and founder of Your Rich BFF. "What you do is put down a security deposit to get approved for a credit card. Your credit limit is the security deposit," says Tu. "The whole point of this to build your credit. If you are able to then make on-time payments, in about six months, you should be able to get approved for a regular, non-secured, beginner credit card."[30]

A limited number of credit card companies, including Bank of America, give the option to apply for a credit card with a co-signer, who agrees to pay off your credit card debt if you are unable, making you a less risky applicant. Students who are ages eighteen to twenty-one and have verifiable income can also often apply and qualify for a student credit card at many companies.

Credit Scores

Paying off your credit card balance every month helps avoid a buildup of debt, but it is important for another reason. Only making the minimum payments required can affect your credit score. Not making payments on time or at all can be even more harmful to your credit score. When you apply for a loan, such as a car loan or student loan, loan companies will look at your credit score. Credit scores are used to determine how likely you are to repay your debt. This in turn will affect whether you get the loan and what the loan terms will be, such as how much interest you will be charged.

The three best-known credit bureaus are Experian, TransUnion, and Equifax. They determine credit scores for individuals using a range of 300 to 850. The low end of the range marks someone as less creditworthy, or less likely to repay debt. The high end of the range marks someone as more creditworthy, or more likely to repay debt.

Credit scores range from 300 to 850, and affect a person's ability to get a loan or other type of credit.

> "Your credit scores can affect whether a lender approves you for a mortgage [home loan], auto loan, personal loan, credit card or other type of credit."[31]
>
> —Colleen McCreary, of Credit Karma

Payment history (for credit cards and existing loans) is an important factor in determining a credit score, but it's not the only consideration. Other factors include how long credit card or loan accounts have been open, how many accounts a person has, and how many new accounts have been opened within the past six to twelve months. A longer credit history can result in a higher score, while opening or applying for many accounts in a short period of time can lower a credit score. In the world of credit, your credit score is critical. "Lower scores typically indicate to lenders that a person is a more risky borrower," says Colleen McCreary of Credit Karma. "Your credit scores can affect whether a lender approves you for a mortgage [home loan], auto loan, personal loan, credit card or other type of credit. And if you're approved, your credit scores also help determine the interest rate and terms you're offered."[31]

While in graduate school, Cassandra Anderson ended up having to rely on credit cards to pay her bills. The resulting debt is a cause of stress, because she worries about both paying off current debt and incurring expenses that could cause it to grow even more. "Currently my credit card debt hasn't impacted any future plans, but it has significantly reduced my credit score,"[32] Anderson says.

Eventually, her low credit score could impact her future plans and goals. A credit report is needed to obtain any kind of loan and can even be checked by potential landlords, insurance companies, utility companies, and employers. This is motivation to start building good credit early. It is also a good reason to avoid piling up debt, which can haunt you for a while through your credit report.

A Realistic View of Debt

Credit card debt is far from the only debt that Americans take on regularly. While you could avoid credit card debt by paying off your balance every month, it is likely that you will obtain some form of debt over the course of your life. The reality is that few people can pay in full for big-ticket purchases such as a new car, a house, or tuition and other expenses for college. Getting a loan to pay for these items isn't inherently bad. What matters is that you can realistically afford whatever it is you're buying. That means making sure you will have the money for monthly loan payments.

It might also mean that you look at more affordable alternatives. Purchasing a used car or choosing a less expensive model can help keep your loan payments lower. In 2025 for instance, Experian reported that the average monthly car payment for new cars was $745 and for used cars $521. Having a strong credit score that will result in a lower interest rate is another way to lower monthly loan payments. Choosing a longer loan term (or number of months or years you have to pay off a loan) can reduce your monthly payment. On the flip side, this will mean paying more

Teens learn woodworking skills at a vocational school. Vocational school can be a way to learn job skills with less debt than a traditional four-year college.

money in the long term due to more time for interest to be added to the loan amount.

A college education is another reason many Americans obtain loans. College can be very expensive. In 2024 *Forbes* reported that over half of students graduate with debt and that the average debt is $28,950. To keep expenses down, some students choose to attend community college for the first two years of their college education or for technical or vocational education programs. Community colleges typically cost less than four-year colleges, so even if a loan is needed, the payments will generally be less.

College loan debt has become a real problem for many people. Some spend decades paying off their student loans. This can be overwhelming and stressful. Kennedy Quintanilla graduated University of Texas at Austin in 2021 with $26,000 in student loan debt. She acknowledges that, as a teen beginning college, she didn't understand the long-term ramifications of student loans. Now she is trying to cut costs to budget for the payments she has to make in order to pay off the loan. That

The Effect of Student Loan Debt on Mental Health

Many high school graduates feel that obtaining a college degree and incurring student loan debt to pay for it is simply what is expected. First-generation college student Maya Chavis financed her college degree with student loans, but now that she has graduated, those looming loan payments cause her anxiety and distress. "It's kind of like a terror type thing. It's always in the back of my mind," Chavis says. "It's a lot to say, okay, like, I'm gonna go talk to somebody about [my anxiety], but to pay $200 for it—that could have been my groceries for the month or I could have paid for my student loans for that month." The rising costs of college and, as a result, student loan debt has organizations like RISE, the nonprofit Chavis works for, advocating for more affordable and accessible college costs.

Quoted in Rainesford Stauffer, "Student Debt Is Taxing Young People's Mental Health," *Teen Vogue*, May 14, 2024. www.teenvogue.com.

process could take ten to fifteen years. She's also trying to determine whether there are ways to make her debt more manageable or pay it off more quickly. "There's so many things that . . . I think even peers my age now don't really understand or have a full grasp on," Quintanilla says. "Things like public service loan forgiveness, income-based repayment, those are all very inaccessible to understand but make a tremendous difference if you operate the system correctly." [33]

Striving to avoid all debt is unrealistic—and even unnecessary. Most people will incur some form of debt during their lives. For teens who want to make wise choices, the best course of action is to learn early about credit and debt. Understanding how credit cards and loans work—including interest rates, fees, and monthly payment options—are all part of this learning. This knowledge can empower you to make your financial goals a reality, without getting bogged down by lots of debt.

CHAPTER FIVE

Financial Fraud and Scams

Holly Johnson is the mother of two teenagers who are fourteen and sixteen years old. They both have already been targets of scammers multiple times through their texts and emails. "My youngest child received almost daily texts from someone who was adamant about getting her Roblox login details so they could 'gift' her some credit for the game, which we monitored and reported until the messages finally stopped,"[34] she recalls. Between their time on social media, apps and online games, teens are frequently victims of scammers looking to trick them into giving up personal financial information or purchasing items that either are knock-offs or don't exist. It's important for teens to learn what these scams look like and what to do when they encounter them.

> "My youngest child received almost daily texts from someone who was adamant about getting her Roblox login details so they could 'gift' her some credit for the game."[34]
>
> —Holly Johnson, mom of teens targeted by scammers

Teens Are a Prime Target for Scammers

Since today's teens have grown up so tech savvy, they often assume they can't be victims of online scams. But in actuality, teens are often targeted specifically by financial scammers because they are spending hours a day on social media and are also sharing more personal information online than any previous generation. A 2023 Deloitte study found that Gen Zers were three times more likely than baby boomers to fall for online scams. While older generations may fall for stereotypical scams over the phone and via email, scammers are pivoting to also target younger people online. Jonathan H. Swanburg, president of TSA Wealth Management, says, “The younger generation may just see an ad on Facebook, or Instagram, or TikTok for some investment that’s going to pay you 10% a month with no risk.”[35] These types of scams require less time investment on the part of the scammers and also can target a lot more people, so it’s not surprising that online scams are becoming more common.

Multiple studies have revealed that those under age thirty are almost as likely to trust what they read on social media as the national news media. Social media is a place that’s ripe for misinformation, which can affect teens’ mental health and self-esteem and also make them vulnerable to falling for scammers posing as legitimate businesses or potential friends. The Federal Bureau of Investigation shared in 2023 that it received 18,174 reports from individuals under age twenty, representing a total loss of $40.7 million.

Teens are often targeted by financial scammers because they spend a lot of time on social media.

"[Teens] are targeted [because] they take longer to find out that they are victims of identity theft, thereby allowing the identity thieves more time to use their identities for criminal purposes."[36]

—Steve Wiseman, scam expert

The previous year's losses were even higher, at $210.5 million. Teens are also more vulnerable to having their identity stolen by scammers, who might use personal information to access bank accounts and medical insurance and to open credit card accounts, says Steve Wiseman, an expert on scams, identity theft, and cybersecurity. "They are targeted for two reasons. The first is that they take longer to find out that they are victims of identity theft, thereby allowing the identity thieves more time to use their identities for criminal purposes." Says Wiseman, "In addition, their information is often used in synthetic identity theft where criminals create a phony identity with information taken from several different people."[36]

Common Scams Targeting Teens

One of the most popular types of scams targeting teens are online shopping scams. A scammer will create an ad for a product or sometimes even an entire website, often paying to boost the ad to make it look more authoritative. Once a teen has paid for the product, they will either never receive it or be sent a knock-off. This is a technique used especially with designer goods and items for occasions when the buyer desires a more unusual or distinct item. Amy Nofziger is director of fraud prevention support at AARP, an organization primarily for older adults. However, AARP also runs a fraud helpline for all ages. Nofziger says the helpline experienced a surge in calls during prom season. Callers reported buying dresses online but never receiving them. "They wanted to wear something that wasn't sold at the mainstream stores, so they ended up placing orders at fake dress shops,"[37] Nofziger says.

Other schemes that teens are especially vulnerable to due to their age are employment, scholarship, and student loan payment scams. These scams attempt to obtain personal information that can then be used to commit identity fraud or to obtain up-front fees or payments for a nonexistent service. These kinds of scams can be sent by email or text or are sometimes contained in online ads. They are often designed to look legitimate by using the student's name. Legitimate offers for jobs or scholarships will never ask for personal information or payment or indicate that you have received a scholarship or won a contest that you never applied for or entered. Employment scams include talent scout scams, in which a scammer will claim they have scouted a teen for modeling, singing, or acting roles but will ask for a fee in advance for their services, headshots, or classes. A legitimate talent scout will not ask for payment in advance and gets paid after you book jobs. A variation on this scam involves placing ads for contests in

Protect Yourself from Identity Theft Online

Revealing too much personal information on social media can leave you vulnerable to scammers, who are happy to use what you share to steal your identity or hack into your financial accounts. Here are some things that experts suggest for teens who want to protect themselves online:

- Don't share your full name, birthday, address, or the school you attend. This information can be used by individuals who could impersonate you to access financial accounts or open new ones in your name. Scammers can also use personal information to pretend to be you and contact friends or family members to scam them as well.
- Check your photos for information they might reveal. Can you see a sign with the name of your school or your house number? Even if you aren't intentionally sharing personal information online, sometimes you can do it by accident, giving scammers opportunities to hack passwords or answers to security questions.
- Review privacy settings to make sure all of your accounts are private and live location is turned off, and never accept friend requests from strangers.
- Use multifactor authentication for your accounts and don't use passwords that include personal information such as names or birthdays; this will make it harder for scammers to access your accounts.

which young people enter their artwork, videos, or writing. Scammers make money by charging entry fees, or by requiring contest winners to pay money in order to collect their awards.

Another tactic used by scammers is to send messages—usually texts, emails, and phone calls—that claim to be from your bank or credit card company and indicate that there has been a breach or another issue with your account. These messages encourage you to click on links within the message or to provide personal information to resolve the issue. Usually, scammers are trying to obtain access to bank and credit card accounts and other personal information that is then used to fraudulently obtain money, loans, or credit card accounts.

Other scammers will spend time trying to build a relationship with the person they are targeting. For example, they might pretend to be a potential friend reaching out in social media private

Online shopping scams are one of the most common types of scams that target teens.

> "I got my best friend dragged into that too and his card was blocked. . . . I can't believe I thought [the scammer] was doing magic tricks. . . . I thought he hacked the system."[38]
>
> —Eman, teen scam victim

messages. In this way, the scammer tries to make the targeted person more comfortable with eventually revealing personal information or clicking on malicious links. Experts say young people, despite having grown up with this technology, are especially vulnerable to email, text, and social media scams.

At age fifteen, Eman fell victim to a social media scam when he saw a fellow Snapchat user's post about money flipping. Money flipping is a scam that promises to invest a small amount of money that will quickly grow into a larger amount. The Snapchat user's video claimed that he would invest $50, which would become $5,000 in no time. Now Eman is embarrassed that he fell for the scam, saying, "Y'all going to think it's so stupid but I was 15 and I fell for it and I wanted money." After Eman provided the scammer with his bank account details, his account was drained. "Those were dark days," he recalls, remembering how passing on the post to his best friend ended with him being scammed as well. "I can't believe I thought [the scammer] was doing magic tricks. . . . I thought he hacked the system."[38]

How to Guard Against Fraud and Scams

Guarding against being a victim of fraud and scams begins by building awareness of the common techniques that scammers use. These techniques are used to trick people into giving money or personal information that scammers can use for hacking into financial accounts or stealing identities to open new accounts. Here are some of the top red flags to identify whether an ad or message is a scam:

- If it seems too good to be true, it probably is. Promises of earning huge amounts of money, an unbelievably good price for an expensive product, or claims of making you into an overnight success or guaranteeing fame and fortune are all suspicious.

- Anyone asking for payment in gift cards or transactions involving cryptocurrency are likely scams.
- Links in messages from a person or company you do not know are likely some form of virus or spyware.
- Requests for personal information such as your address, Social Security number, or bank account information, even if it looks like it is coming from an official source, are signs that a scammer might be trying to steal your identity.
- Listen to your gut. If you feel like something feels wrong, it most likely is.

Most of all, it is important to stop and think before responding to a social media message from someone you don't know or before making a purchase. Ben Colman of the cybersecurity firm

Financial Sextortion

Considered the fastest-growing cybercrime that targets children and teens, financial sextortion scams mostly target teenage boys. In 2023 the Federal Bureau of Investigation released a public safety report about financial sextortion after receiving reports about three thousand minors who were victims in the previous year. These crimes begin when a scammer, usually impersonating a teenage girl, builds a relationship with the victim before encouraging the teen to send them nude photos or engage in sexual conversations. Then the scammer will blackmail the teen, threatening to release the photos or content of their conversations and shaming them. They generally will ask for gift cards or money through peer-to-peer payment apps. While the ramifications can be financial, these kind of scams also have a very real impact on the mental health of teens. Jennifer Butta's son killed himself after being subjected to financial sextortion. Butta wants teens to know: "You may feel humiliated, but life will go on. It is so much better to seek out that help, because it's a situation that you're not prepared to handle on your own."

Quoted in Rachel Hale, "These Teenage Boys Were Blackmailed Online–and It Cost Them Their Lives," *USA Today*, February 25, 2025. www.usatoday.com.

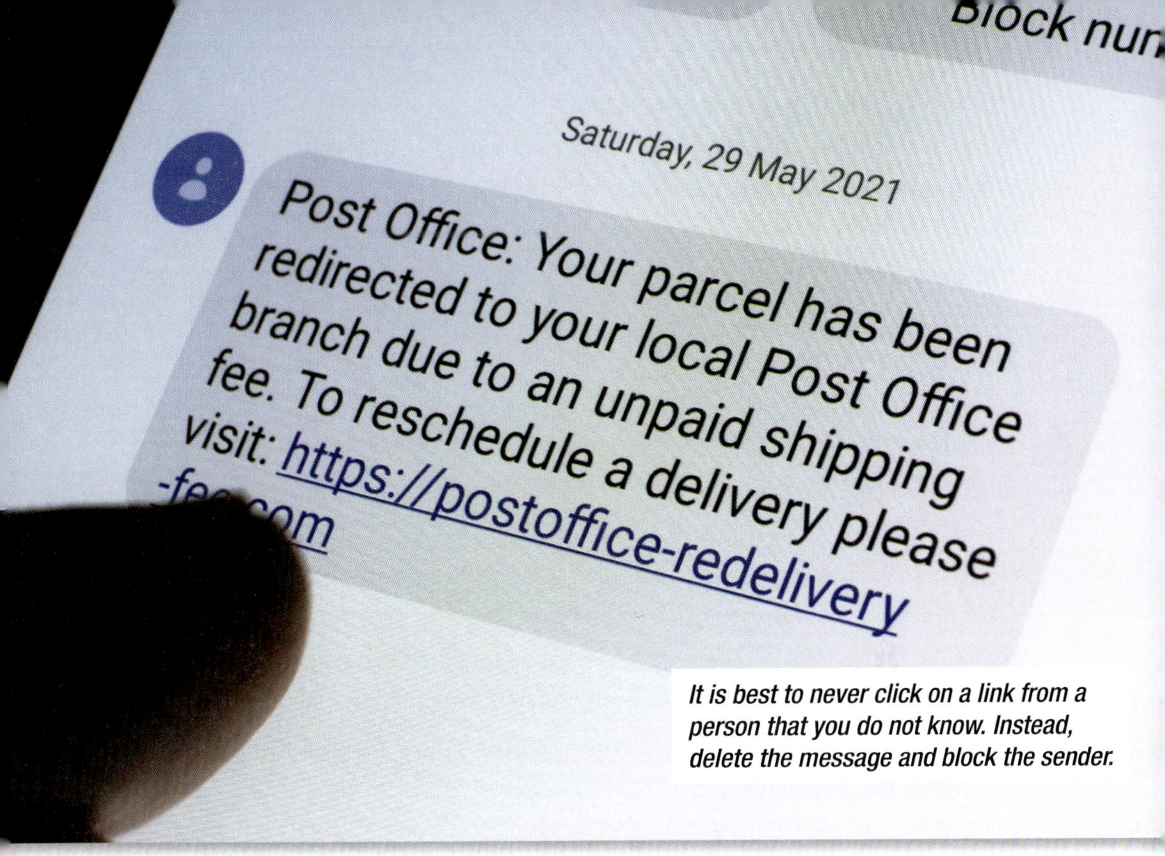

It is best to never click on a link from a person that you do not know. Instead, delete the message and block the sender.

Reality Defender recommends that teens utilize the THINK method before responding to messages. This involves asking whether the message is true, helpful, inspiring, necessary, and kind.

Colman says, "This helps them pause before engaging."[39] He recommends that teens verify that the company or individual sending a message or posting an advertisement is who they say they are before responding or making a purchase. This should be done, not by clicking on a link in the message or ad, but by using your own phone or computer browser. As a rule, it is best simply to not click on any links sent from senders that you do not know personally and also not respond to messages sent by strangers. Deleting these messages—whether they arrive as emails, texts, or social media private messages—and either blocking the sender or reporting the messages as spam are best practices.

Being aware of common scammer tactics is another good way to avoid them. A scam email or text message claiming to originate from an official source such as your bank might ask for your personal or financial information. This should be viewed as a big red flag because financial institutions will never ask clients to provide this information by message. Other red flags include the sender not having an official company email address, a messaged addressed to "undisclosed-recipients," or not addressed to you personally.

If something feels or looks off, have a conversation about it with a trusted adult. They can also assist in researching a website, company, or ad before making a purchase to determine whether you would be purchasing from a legitimate site. Search for the company name accompanied by "reviews," "scam," or "fraud" to see if any other shoppers have reported problems. If the company has a website you can also type in the URL on the online identity provider website Whois.com to see whether anything suspicious comes up. Sometimes scammers even try to use the name of a legitimate store and create a copy of its website to trick people into making purchases. "If you go and find that the 'Walmart' website has only been up for about a week," says Weisman, "or that it's registered to someone in North Korea, you've got a pretty good idea that it's a scam."[40]

While taking measures to prevent becoming the victim of a scammer is important, it does still happen to thousands of American teens and adults every year. It can be embarrassing and leave a victim feeling vulnerable, but it is important to share what has happened with an adult immediately. They can help take the appropriate next steps, which may include filing a fraud report with the bank or credit card company, changing passwords, placing a fraud alert with credit bureaus, and freezing your credit report so scammers cannot open any new accounts in your name.

Teens are living their lives online more than any other previous generations, which makes them vulnerable to scammers who now utilize social media, text messages, and games to target victims. However, with knowledge, teens can recognize potential scams and know the next steps to take if they encounter a scam online.

SOURCE NOTES

Introduction: Why Learn About Personal Finance?

1. Quoted in Sara Li, "How Financial Stress Is Impacting Young People's Mental Health," *Teen Vogue*, November 11, 2021. www.teenvogue.com.
2. Jamie Hanson, "Teenagers Often Know When Their Parents Are Having Money Problems," The Conversation, March 8, 2024. https://theconversation.com.
3. Quoted in Elizabeth Ayoola, "How to Uncover and Address Your Teen's Money Fears," NerdWallet, June 12, 2023. www.nerdwallet.com.
4. Quoted in Roxana Popescu, "Teens Want Concert Tickets, Target Runs and Food," *San Diego (CA) Union-Tribune*, October 28, 2024. www.sandiegouniontribune.com.

Chapter One: How to Budget

5. Quoted in Donnavan Smoot, "Young People Are Overspending Online. How Social Media and 'Buy Now, Pay Later' Apps Play a Big Role," Yahoo! News, April 16, 2024. www.yahoo.com.
6. Quoted in Smoot, "Young People Are Overspending Online."
7. Anastasia Micich, "Breaking Down the Relationship Between Brands and Teens," Truth in Advertising, August 19, 2024. https://truthinadvertising.org.
8. Quoted in Popescu, "Teens Want Concert Tickets, Target Runs and Food."
9. Erin Gobler, "Budgeting for Teens: How to Get Started," Clever Girl Finance, January 5, 2025. www.clevergirlfinance.com.
10. Brad Hanson, "Budgeting for Teens: 18 Tips for Growing Your Money Young," Credit Karma, February 22, 2024. www.creditkarma.com.

Chapter Two: How to Save Money

11. Ashley Eli, *How I Bought First Car at 16*, YouTube, June 1, 2023. www.youtube.com/watch?v=7SW2r0apxa4.
12. Quoted in Hannah Oh, "Here Are 14 Handy Tricks for Saving Money in College (Yes, It's Possible)," *Seventeen*, November 15, 2022. www.seventeen.com.

13. Quoted in Hannah Oh, "13 Ways for Teenagers to Save Money with (or Without) a Job," *Seventeen*, August 11, 2022. www.seventeen.com.
14. Truly Paula, *How to Save Money as a Teenager & Young Adult in 2023*, YouTube, March 12, 2022. www.youtube.com/watch?v=kTEISMO4zS4&t=2s.
15. Quoted in Oh, "13 Ways for Teenagers to Save Money with (or Without) a Job."
16. Jamela Adam, "American Savings by Generation: How Balances and Goals Vary by Age," *Forbes*, August 15, 2024. www.forbes.com.

Chapter Three: How to Invest and Grow Your Money

17. Quoted in Ryan Ermey, "Investing for Teens: How to Get Started," Acorns, August 25, 2022. www.acorns.com.
18. Quoted in Agustin Hays, "This High School Junior Bought 3 Stocks When She Was 14 Years Old, Then Purchased a Tesla," Fox Business, February 26, 2024. www.foxbusiness.com.
19. Quoted in Nasdaq, "Investing for Teens: Most Teens Want to Invest (but Aren't)," September 9, 2023. www.nasdaq.com.
20. Quoted in Nasdaq, "Investing for Teens."
21. Quoted in Hannah Miao and Gunjan Banerji, "These Teenagers Know More About Investing than You Do," *Wall Street Journal*, February 18, 2024. www.wsj.com.
22. Quoted in Miao and Banerji, "These Teenagers Know More About Investing than You Do."
23. Quoted in Hannah Oh, "How to Confidently Invest Your Money (a Guide for Beginners)," *Seventeen*, April 12, 2023. www.seventeen.com.
24. Gina Young, "You Can Give Your Teenager a Massive (Tax-Free) Retirement Boost—Here's What the Law Allows," Investopedia, June 26, 2025. www.investopedia.com.
25. Quoted in Oh, "How to Confidently Invest Your Money (a Guide for Beginners)."
26. Quoted in Ermey, "Investing for Teens."

Chapter Four: All About Credit and Debt

27. Quoted in Jacqui Germain, "Young People and Credit Card Debt: How Small Loans Can Spiral," *Teen Vogue*, January 25, 2021. www.teenvogue.com.

28. Quoted in Germain, “Young People and Credit Card Debt.”
29. Hannah Oh, “Everything You Need to Know About Credit Cards for Teens,” *Seventeen*, August 9, 2022. www.seventeen.com.
30. Quoted in Oh, “Everything You Need to Know About Credit Cards for Teens.”
31. Quoted in Oh, “Everything You Need to Know About Credit Cards for Teens.”
32. Quoted in Germain, “Young People and Credit Card Debt.”
33. Quoted in Katie Kindelan, “Gen Z Is Burdened by Student Loan Debt, and Now Many Are Facing Payments for 1st Time,” ABC News, September 29, 2023. https://abcnews.go.com.

Chapter Five: Financial Fraud and Scams

34. Holly Johnson, “My Kids Were Targeted by Scams. Here’s How I Keep Them Safe,” CNET, April 21, 2025. www.cnet.com.
35. Quoted in Solcyré Burga, “Why Gen Z Is Surprisingly Susceptible to Financial Scams,” *Time*, February 24, 2024. https://time.com.
36. Quoted in Janet Fowler, “10 Common Scams Targeted at Teens,” Investopedia, November 27, 2022. www.investopedia.com.
37. Quoted in Christina Ianzito, “Criminals Increasingly Target Teens for Sextortion and Other Online Scams,” AARP, June 7, 2023. www.aarp.org.
38. SavedEman Live, *Exposing How I Got Scammed as a Teen*, YouTube. June 25, 2025. www.youtube.com/watch?v=cyyL6hd5xJA.
39. Johnson, “My Kids Were Targeted by Scams.”
40. Quoted in Ianzito, “Criminals Increasingly Target Teens for Sextortion and Other Online Scams.”

Federal Bureau of Investigation (FBI)

www.fbi.gov/how-we-can-help-you/scams-and-safety/common-frauds-and-scams

The FBI is the federal agency responsible for investigating many frauds and scams targeting Americans. Its website offers information about common frauds and scams and how to file a report if you are the victim of one.

Fidelity

www.fidelity.com/learning-center/overview

Fidelity is a top brokerage firm, but it also offers a robust learning center breaking down financial topics in easy-to-understand terms. Articles, videos, and webinars provide knowledge about terminology, how to invest, and how to best prepare for your financial future.

National Endowment for Financial Education

www.nefe.org

This organization is focused on increasing financial literacy for Americans. It does this by supporting research on personal finance education, exploring how K–12 schools can integrate personal finance into their curriculum, and facilitating gatherings for researchers, educators, and policymakers in the personal finance sphere.

Stock Market Game

www.stockmarketgame.org

The Stock Market Game gives teens the opportunity to learn all about the stock market without any real risk involved, because they are playing with pretend money. Teens can learn individually, with friends, or as part of an after-school club. An adult must sign up for an account for those under age eighteen.

Youth for Finance

www.youthforfinance.org

This nonprofit based in California is focused on bringing financial education to underprivileged youth in the United States and around the world. It helps teens start their own chapters to facilitate learning with a stock market simulator game and a thirty-week economics curriculum, among other resources.

FOR FURTHER RESEARCH

Books

Emma Davis, *Personal Finance for Teens: The Ultimate Guide to Transforming Your Financial Game at a Young Age—Learn, Earn, and Invest to Grow Your Wealth.* Impact, 2024.

Barbara Diggs, *Teen Guide to Managing Money*. ReferencePoint, 2025.

Morgan Housel, *The Psychology of Money: Timeless Lessons on Wealth, Greed, and Happiness.* Harriman House, 2020.

Jack Rosenthal. *Teen Investing 101: 101 of the Most Important Financial Literacy Terms.* Published by the author, 2021.

Dan Sheeks, *First to a Million: A Teenager's Guide to Achieving Early Financial Independence.* BiggerPockets, 2021.

Tom Streissguth, *How Does Investing Work?* ReferencePoint, 2023.

Bola Sukunbi, *The Side Hustle Guide: Build a Successful Side Hustle and Increase Your Income.* Wiley, 2021.

Internet Sources

Anastasia Micich, "Breaking Down the Relationship Between Brands and Teens," Truth in Advertising, August 19, 2024. https://truthinadvertising.org.

MoneyWise, "54 Eye-Opening Personal Finance Statistics and Facts in 2025," February 11, 2025. https://moneywise.com.

Hannah Oh, "Here Are 14 Handy Tricks for Saving Money in College (Yes, It's Possible)," *Seventeen*, November 15, 2022. www.seventeen.com.

R.J. Weiss, "I'm a CFP® and Parent—My Review of the Best Banking & Investing Apps for Kids," Ways to Wealth, January 28, 2025. www.thewaystowealth.com.

INDEX

PICTURE CREDITS

Cover: Shutterstock.com

6: fizkes/Shutterstock
10: Ground Picture/Shutterstock
13: fizkes/Shutterstock
15: Matinee Duangphet/iStockphoto
18: Orlando Arce/Shutterstock
21: NicOStudio/Shutterstock
23: Lopolo/Shutterstock
26: BearFotos/Shutterstock
29: Art Genie/Shutterstock
33: pics five/Shutterstock
37: Trzykropy/Shutterstock
39: Tolgart/iStockphoto
41: Phovoir/Shutterstock
45: Pixel-Shot/Shutterstock
48: Daniel_Dash/Shutterstock
51: Mundissima/Shutterstock

ABOUT THE AUTHOR

Sara Rowe Mount writes articles and books for children and teens. She lives in the Northeast with her husband, their daughter, and lots of books.